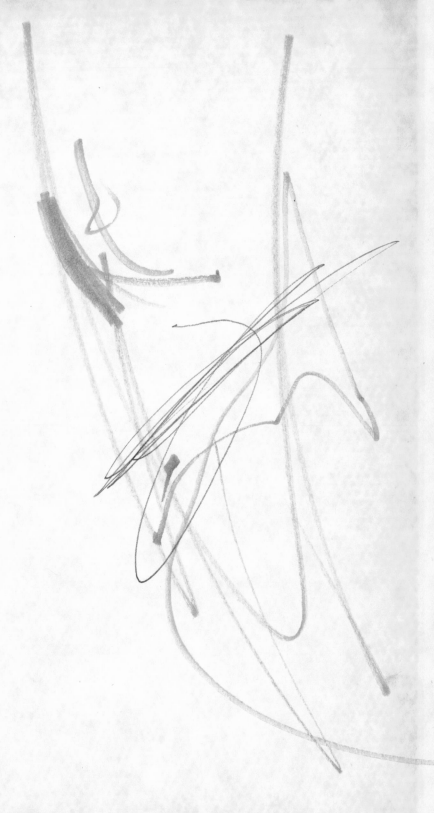

Disney's Year Book 1991

Disney's Year Book 1991

GROLIER ENTERPRISES INC.
Danbury, Connecticut

FERN L. MAMBERG   *Executive Editor*
DON LONGABUCCO   *Art Director*
MARILYN SMITH   *Production Manager*

ISBN: 0-7172-8254-6
ISSN: 0273-1274

Illustration Credits and Acknowledgments

6—© Bob Winsett/Profiles West; 7—Artist, Michèle A. McLean; 8—© Chris Luneski/Image Cascade; 9—Theodore L. Manekin; Theodore L. Manekin; Theodore L. Manekin; © Chris Luneski/Image Cascade; 8–9—Theodore L. Manekin; 10–11—Jackie Geyer/Ranger Rick; 24—© Dave B. Fleetham/Tom Stack & Associates; 25—© Larry Lipsky/DRK Photo; 26—© James H. Carmichael/Bruce Coleman Inc.; 27—© Stephen J. Krasemann/DRK Photo; 28—© Ed Robinson/Tom Stack & Associates; 29—© Fred Bavendam/Valan Photos; 30–31—Designed and created by Michèle A. McLean; 32–33—© Co Rentmeester; 33—The Granger Collection; 34—© Linda Hill; 35—Chad Slattery; 48–49—© Tobey Sanford; 50—Martin Rogers/Stock Boston; 51–52—© John P. Kelly/The Image Bank; 53—© Mark McKenna; 54–55—Peach Reynolds; 68–69—John Running/Black Star; 70—The Granger Collection; 71—Historical Picture Service; 72—Illinois State Historical Library; Culver Pictures; 73—Museum of the Confederacy; 74—The Granger Collection; 75—Historical Picture Service; 76—© Chad Slattery; 77—© Jerry Howard/Positive Images; 90—© Robert A. Tyrell; 91—© Clayton A. Fogle; © Robert A. Tyrell; 92—Artist, Michèle A. McLean; 93—© Clayton A. Fogle; 94—© Caroline Wood/F-Stock; 95—© Nathan Bilow/Allsport.

Contents

GO FLY A KITE

If you look up and see a huge butterfly fluttering over your head, don't worry. It's not a giant insect. Chances are you're seeing a kite. Kite flying is more popular today than ever before. And beautiful kites shaped like butterflies—and many other things—can often be seen floating in the air on breezy days.

Kites aren't a recent creation. They were probably invented in China more than 2,000 years ago! According to one legend, a farmer got the idea when a gust of wind blew his hat off. He didn't lose his hat because it had a string that was tied under his chin. But the farmer saw that the wind could carry his hat away. And this, so the story goes, gave him an idea for a wonderful toy.

In the past, kites weren't just toys. For example, kites were used during wars to scatter leaflets over enemy troops. Some very large kites even carried soldiers into the sky so they could watch enemy troops. Other kites were used to send weather instruments high above earth. But today most kites are flown just for the fun of it.

These popular toys come in every color of the rainbow, and many are decorated with fantastic designs. They are so colorful that some people call kite flying "painting the sky." Kites also come in all shapes and sizes. The diamond-shaped kite is probably the most familiar. But kites are also shaped like butterflies, dragons, birds, flowers, and centipedes.

Kiting Tips

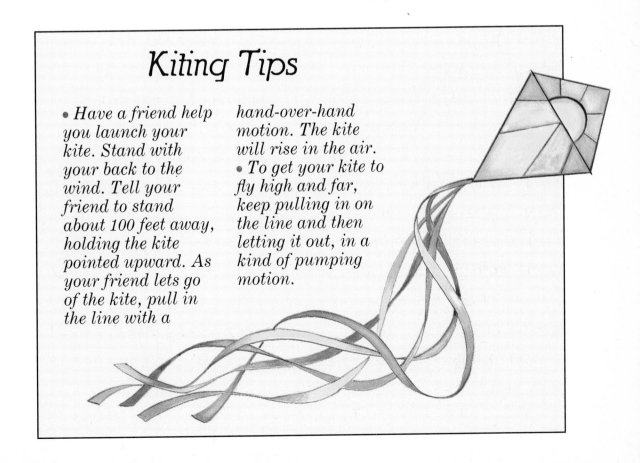

- *Have a friend help you launch your kite. Stand with your back to the wind. Tell your friend to stand about 100 feet away, holding the kite pointed upward. As your friend lets go of the kite, pull in the line with a hand-over-hand motion. The kite will rise in the air.*
- *To get your kite to fly high and far, keep pulling in on the line and then letting it out, in a kind of pumping motion.*

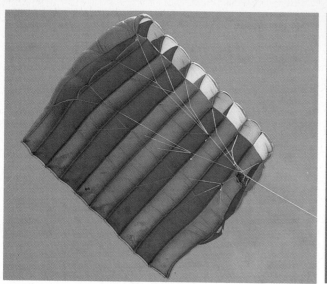
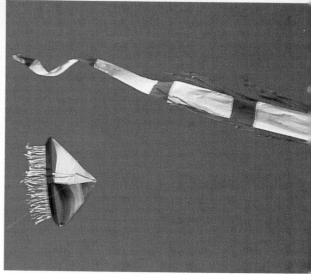

All kites have three basic parts. The **wing surface**—the kite itself—is the part that's lifted by the wind. The **flying line** is used to control the flight of the kite. And it keeps the kite from blowing away. The **bridle** connects the flying line to the kite. It also holds the face of the kite at an angle to the wind.

Many people like to build their own kites. If you do this, use the lightest material possible. The heavier the material, the more it will pull the kite down. The wing can be made from paper, cloth, or plastic. The wing's supporting frame is made of wood. Use wood that's light, strong, and flexible. Use strong string for the flying line. Linen cord, fishing line, or braided nylon are good for this. The bridle can be made from ordinary string or thin cord. And keep in mind that for a kite to stay in the air it should be symmetrical—each side should be similar to the other. MOST IMPORTANT: Never use metal in any part of your kite. Metal conducts electricity, and you could get a shock.

Whether you build your own kite or buy one, you'll be sure to enjoy "painting the sky."

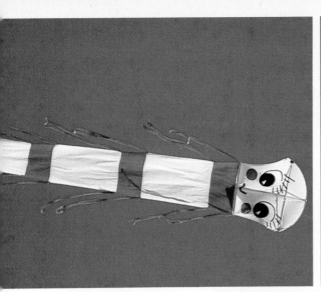
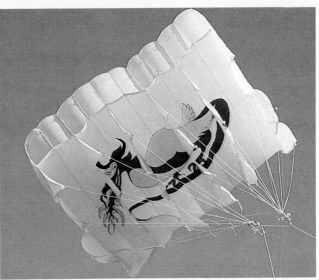

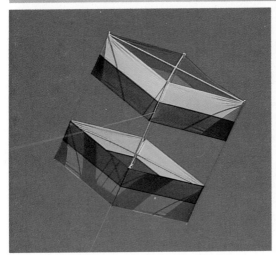

WHAT COULD IT BE?

Is it a creature put together by a mad scientist? No! It's a mystery creature made up of parts of real animals. Find each of the numbered parts and guess what animal it comes from.

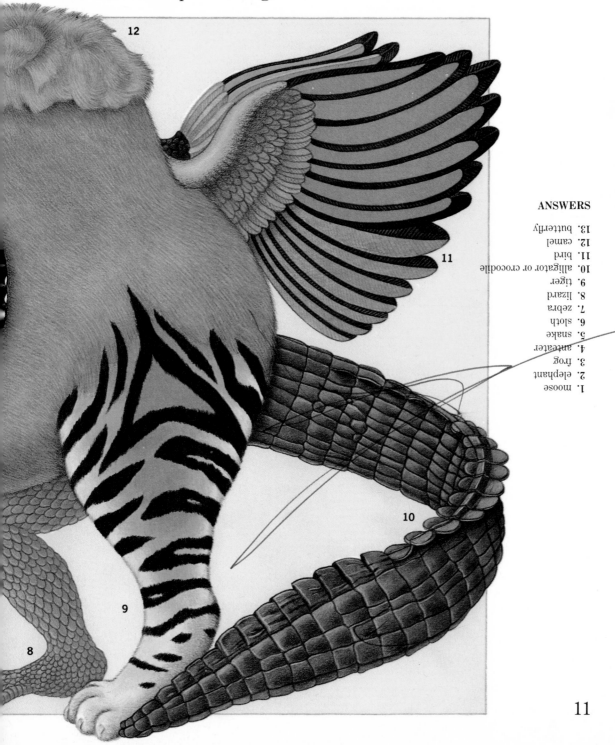

THE DOUBTING DALMATIAN

Outside it was a dark and stormy London night, but indoors a warm fire blazed. Fifteen Dalmatian puppies were watching a program about a famous English detective who was very good at solving crimes.

The smallest puppy was barking at the screen.

"Lucky, do pipe down! We can't hear a thing," said Nanny kindly. She was perched on the edge of her chair, knitting a sock for her employer, Roger Radcliffe.

Suddenly the puppies yelped and dove under Nanny's chair. "Silly puppies!" Nanny laughed. "That was only a lightning flash." Then a clap of thunder shook the house, and the lights went out!

"Don't worry, little ones," said Nanny. "I'll just get some candles, and we'll all be right as rain."

Freckles shivered under the chair in the dark. "I just wish mom and dad hadn't gone on holiday with Roger and Anita," she said.

"Me, too," sighed her brother Rolly. "They won't be back until tomorrow."

A light flickered on the far side of the room as Nanny lit the candle. The light made the puppies feel braver, and one by one they crawled out from under the chair.

Lightning flashed again. Nanny raised her candle toward the window in the front door and gasped. There was someone at the door. Lucky growled low in his throat, and the other puppies pushed up close to Nanny. The doorbell rang.

"Who's there?" called Nanny fearfully.

"It's Anita's Aunt Ida. From America," said a woman's voice. "Please let me in."

Nanny opened the door. Lucky growled again as a tall, dripping form in a tweed coat, carrying two huge suitcases, rushed into the hall. Aunt Ida—or whoever she was—set her dripping bags down, plopped herself on the stairs, and began

pulling off a huge pair of black rubber boots.

"Didn't Anita tell you I was coming?" she asked. "I wrote to her over a month ago. She wrote back saying she'd love to have me

stay." The mysterious woman dug around in her purse and took out a letter.

Nanny studied it closely in the candlelight. "This doesn't say when," she said suspiciously.

"Two weeks ago I sent Anita a postcard, telling her I would arrive tonight."

"Well," said Nanny, "I'm sure she didn't know you were coming. You see, she and Master Roger have gone camping. There's no way to phone, but she'll be home tomorrow. I suppose you can stay here tonight. Meanwhile, would you like a cup of tea?"

"That would be lovely," said the stranger, and she followed Nanny into the kitchen, trailed by a crowd of curious puppies.

Suddenly the lights came back on. "Thank goodness!" said Rolly. He joined Lucky and Patch, who had stayed behind in the hallway to sniff Aunt Ida's wet suitcases and big rubber boots.

"She's not Anita's aunt from America!" said Lucky.

"Why not?" asked Patch. "Nanny believes her. And what about that letter from Anita?"

"She wrote it herself!" said Lucky.

"She sounds American," said Rolly.

"She's faking," Lucky stated.

16

"Then who is she?" asked Patch.

"Elementary, my dear brother," began Lucky. "Let's figure it out from the clues."

"Oh, I get it," said Rolly. "Like the detective on television. Okay. What's the first clue?"

Lucky sniffed again at her boots. "These boots. They aren't American. They're Wellington boots, made in England. And that coat is made of English tweed. I don't think Aunt Ida is from America at all!"

"Well, if she's not Anita's Aunt Ida from America, then who is she?" Patch asked.

Lucky looked at Aunt Ida's biggest suitcase. "Aunt Ida said she had been traveling around England," he said. "This is a bus tag, but it only says 'London.' If she'd been all over, lots of towns would be listed on it."

Patch and Rolly dashed across the room. They thought they had discovered a crime. In his excitement, Rolly knocked into the big suitcase. It clattered loudly as it rocked back and forth.

Aunt Ida came running. She opened the bag, looked inside, and then closed it again.

"No harm done, Nanny," she called. "One of your puppies must have knocked it over." She went back to the kitchen.

"Did you see that?" yelped Lucky. He was so excited he could hardly talk. "That bag was full of valuable china. I bet Aunt Ida is a cat burglar. She gets into people's homes with a made-up story about being someone's aunt and robs them at night when they're asleep."

"Oh, no!" cried Patch. "What should we do now?"

"We'll stand guard outside her door tonight. If she gets up, we'll bark."

When Roger and Anita returned home early the next morning with Pongo and Perdita, the puppies' parents, they found twelve

puppies asleep in a warm basket by the stove. And they found
Lucky, Patch, and Rolly asleep in front of the door to Aunt Ida's
room.

Later that day, Lucky explained to his mother and father about
the strange Aunt Ida, and why
they had slept in front of her
door.

"Silly puppies," said Perdita.
"Aunt Ida just told Anita she

bought the dishes yesterday. She had to get a new bag to carry them, so the tag only said 'London.' "

"What about the English clothes?" asked Lucky.

"She bought the coat and boots here," said his mother.

"You know, Lucky," said his father, "it's okay to be suspicious of strangers, but it's not a good idea to jump to conclusions."

"I guess you're right," said Lucky. "But there's still one mystery we haven't solved."

"What's that?" asked his father.

"Why didn't Anita ever get the card Aunt Ida sent?"

"Someone—a puppy perhaps—must have picked it up," said his mother.

"You mean one of us chewed up the postcard?"

"I'm afraid so," she said.

"Was it a pretty picture card that smelled like flowers?" Rolly asked, looking guilty.

"Oh, Rolly!" sighed Lucky.

"Well, I was hungry!" Rolly said.

Lucky chuckled. "Oh, well," he said, "it was fun playing detective for one night, anyway."

The clownfish–sea anemone partnership helps them both to survive.

ANIMAL PARTNERS

Having a partner is great—he or she is always there to help you out. And in return, you can help your partner. When we think of partners, we usually think of people helping people. But many different kinds of animals have partners, too.

You have probably seen cats, monkeys, and other animals cleaning themselves. But there are many animals that can't clean themselves. So they rely on partners to do it for them. The sea anemone and the clownfish have a partnership like this.

Sea anemones are animals that look like flowers. They have dozens of brightly colored tentacles that wave about in the water. The tentacles have poisonous stingers, and the anemones use them to kill fish for food. But there's one fish that it doesn't kill. Clownfish are able to live right among the tentacles without being harmed! The clownfish helps the anemones by cleaning away dirt and tiny creatures of the sea from among the tentacles. In return,

This cleaner shrimp isn't afraid of its much larger partner.

the clownfish gets a meal. It also gets protection—few enemies will chase the clownfish and risk the anemone's sting.

The cleaner shrimp and a number of large fish have a similar partnership. The cleaner shrimp sets up a kind of cleaning station in the ocean. Large fish line up there, waiting their turn to be cleaned. Many of the fish that are about to be cleaned will eat just about anything that moves. But they almost never eat the cleaner shrimp. As the large fish wait calmly, the little cleaner shrimp picks them clean—and gets a free meal at the same time.

Many other ocean creatures perform cleaning services. One of them is the remora, or suckerfish. This bold fish travels with the

The remora cleans the shark and gets food and protection in return.

A rhino helps egrets catch food, and the egrets warn the rhino of danger.

shark, one of the most feared fish of the ocean. The remora has a large sucker on top of its head. It uses this to attach itself to the shark. (Some remoras attach themselves to turtles and whales.) As the shark swims along, the remora travels all over its body, removing dirt. It gets food and protection—and an occasional feast. Sharks are messy eaters. When the shark feeds, the remora detaches itself and gobbles up the leftover bits.

Some birds have partnerships, too. One of the most familiar of these is the cattle egret. In Africa, this snowy white bird can be seen hopping around the feet of antelopes, zebras, elephants, and other large animals. In the Americas, it can be seen among herds of cattle. These large animals help the egret catch its food. The egret eats insects, especially grasshoppers. As the large animals move through the grass, they disturb the insects that are hiding

The sponge crab's sponge "hat" helps the crab hide from its enemies. And as the crab moves along, the sponge gets a steady supply of food.

there. The insects pop up into the air. The egret spots them and gobbles them up. What does the egret do for the large animals? It acts as a guard and warns them of approaching danger. It does this by hopping up on the animal's back, calling, and flapping its wings. If the animal doesn't take notice right away, the egret will even peck it on its head to get its attention.

Many ocean animals also team up for defense. Among them are certain crabs and sponges. The crab, as you might guess, is called the sponge crab. It looks around until it finds the right kind of sponge. Then the crab snips off a piece of the sponge with its claws. It puts the sponge on top of its shell and holds it there with its back legs. The sponge grows along with the crab. It eventually covers the crab's shell completely. This hides the crab from any other sea animals that might want to eat it. But the sponge isn't along just for the ride. Sponges filter tiny pieces of food from the water. As the crab moves along the ocean floor, food-filled water passes through the sponge, giving it a steady supply of food.

Other crabs team up with anemones. One of these is the pom-pom crab. It carries anemones in its claws. If an enemy comes near, the crab stretches out its claws and threatens the attacker with an anemone sting. What does the anemone get for being the crab's weapon? The slow-moving anemone gets a fast—and free—ride to a new and richer feeding ground. And because crabs are such messy eaters, the anemone may even be able to pick up some scraps from the crab's meal.

The pom-pom crab carries sea anemones like a cheerleader carries pom-poms. But the crab's "pom-poms" are armed with deadly stingers.

LEAF ART:
Don't Waste Them, Paste Them!

You can make birds, fish, and other animals out of leaves. First, collect different kinds of leaves. Then dry them. To do this, put them between sheets of newspaper and place them under a stack of heavy books for several days. Now design your animals. Glue or paste each leaf in place.

THE THRILL OF THE RIDE

Slowly the car climbs higher and higher. It's above the treetops now, supported only by a spindly wooden frame. Your heart is beating faster, and your palms begin to sweat. Something dreadful is about to happen!

Suddenly, the car swings around a bend. It takes you over the top and plunges down toward the ground at frightening speed. The wind whips your hair back and brings tears to your eyes. Your stomach is in your throat and your heart is in your knees. Your mouth is wide open, and you're screaming for all you are worth.

And you love every minute of it!

For sheer thrills and terrifying chills, nothing beats a roller coaster. These exciting rides have been around for about three

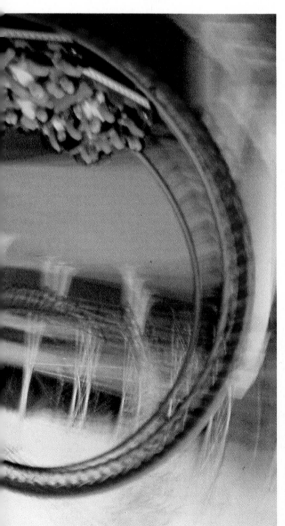

Riders paid only a nickel to ride the first Coney Island coaster in Brooklyn, New York, in 1884 (below). Today's roller coasters (left) are more expensive—but people still find them to be a scream!

hundred years. The Russians came up with the basic idea. Their first coasters were actually ice slides. The slides provided a slick, fast surface for sleds. Riders climbed to a platform at the top and then shot straight down at thrilling speeds. The French added tiny wheels to the sleds in the 1800's. Ice wasn't needed, so the slides could be enjoyed year-round.

The first U.S. coaster was built in the late 1800's. It was actually a railway that had been changed into a fun ride. It carried people to the top of a mountain and then sent them down again—at 5 miles an hour. Compare that to today's coasters. Some of them go more than 50 miles an hour!

The speed of a roller coaster will keep you glued to your seat.

Left: The Magnum XL-200 coaster plunges a frightening 20 stories.
Right: On King Cobra, riders stand up during the entire looping ride.

Today's roller coasters aren't just fast. They take thrillseekers
as high as a 20-story building. Then they plunge toward the
earth, speeding through turns, corkscrews, spirals, and complete
loops. Some coasters even carry riders standing up—they are
strapped into cushioned harnesses.

Old or new, it seems that just about everyone loves a roller
coaster ride. What heart-stopping twist will coaster designers
think up next? Whatever it is, one thing is certain. People will
line up for a chance to feel the thrill of the ride.

35

MILLION-DOLLAR DOLLS

On a foggy afternoon in London, Basil the Great Mouse Detective and Doctor David Q. Dawson were admiring a gift from Hiram Flaversham, the toymaker they had once rescued from Professor Ratigan. Flaversham had sent Basil a wonderful invention that cleaned and refilled his pipe.

Suddenly they heard someone stomping up the stairs. "Out of my way!" cried a voice. "Only the Great Mouse Detective can help me!"

In burst a woman, waving a handkerchief and panting for breath. The woman blew her nose and started talking. "Last night someone broke into my house and stole my sapphires! I'm sure the thief is selling them this very instant!"

"There, there," said the doctor soothingly. "Calm yourself, Madame. Basil needs to ask some questions."

"I have all the information I need," said Basil. "The woman before us is Countess Zenobia, who lives in a mansion on Hampstead Heath. She has an old Irish setter, and she leaves a back door open at night for the dog. Last night, a thief entered through that very door and stole the sapphires."

"I say!" exclaimed Doctor Dawson. "How did you figure all that out?"

"Elementary, my dear Dawson," said Basil. "Our guest must have an elderly Irish setter—there are red and gray dog hairs on the hem of her dress. No doubt she gives it complete freedom of

the house and yard. She also has the sniffles, which leads me to believe that she caught cold from leaving the back door open."

"But how do you know my name?" asked the woman.

"I noticed that you had the initial 'Z' on your locket," said Basil. "You aren't married, since you wear no wedding ring, so it must be your first name that begins with a Z. I read in the newspaper this morning about a Countess Zenobia, who had recently bought a mansion on Hampstead Heath."

"That's all very smart of you," sniffed the countess, "but can you help me find my jewels?"

"I will try, Madame," answered Basil. "Take us to the scene of the crime."

When they got to the countess's mansion, Basil asked, "Madame, where did you keep the jewels?"

"In my dressing room," she said. "I'll show you."

The countess and Dawson watched Basil search the dressing room. "Do you see anything?" asked Dawson.

"This is strange," said Basil. "The countess's high heels have left marks on the rug, but no one else has stepped on it. It's almost as if the thief flew in!"

Basil stood up suddenly. When Doctor Dawson saw the look on Basil's face, he cried, "No! It can't be!"

40

"It can't be what?" cried the countess.

"Fidget, Madame!" replied Basil. "An evil bat who works for an even more evil rat!"

"Come," Basil added. "We must check the backyard for clues."

Dawson and the countess followed Basil into the yard. There the detective found a tiny dancing doll.

"I say," fretted the doctor, "doesn't that look like Olivia Flaversham's doll?"

"Indeed it does," replied Basil. "We must hurry to Flaversham's toy shop. I fear for our friends!"

Leaving the countess behind, Basil and Dawson hurried to the toy shop. Flaversham opened the door. "Basil!" he cried. "I'm so happy to see you!"

The detective pushed his way into the room. "Forgive my poor manners," he said, "but I had to make sure that you and Olivia were all right. Where is your daughter, by the way?"

"With a friend," Flaversham said. "What's wrong?"

As Basil was about to explain, he noticed an object across the room. It was a doll with no eyes. "Why doesn't that doll have eyes?" the detective asked.

"I haven't put them in yet," said Flaversham.

Basil frowned, and then asked,

sapphires that were stolen from Countess Zenobia last night. How did you get them?"

Flaversham explained. "A fellow came into my shop this morning and gave me these eyes to put in some dolls I'm to make for . . ."

"Me!" came a

"You weren't planning to put in blue eyes, were you?"

"Why, yes," answered Flaversham. "How did you guess?"

"May I see those blue eyes?" asked Basil.

Puzzled, Flaversham went to his workshop and returned with a handful of blue objects. "They're made of glass," he said, "but they shine like jewels."

"They *are* jewels," Basil announced. "They're the

voice from the door. They whirled around to see a familiar figure.

"Ratigan!" cried Basil. "I might have known!"

"Yes, it is I!" sneered the professor.

"So it was you who asked me to make dancing dolls for the poor children of Adzharia!" cried Flaversham.

"Very clever, Ratigan," said Basil. "You smuggle the jewels

out of the country in dolls. Isn't that rather tame for a master criminal?"

"Tame or not, Basil," chuckled Ratigan, "I don't plan to stop with these little sapphires. My next target will be the Crown Jewels! And I'll have no trouble stealing them—once *you're* out of the way!"

"You monster!" cried Dawson.

"You fool!" added Flaversham, and he knocked down one of

Ratigan's men and ran for the door. When Ratigan tried to catch him, Flaversham threw the sapphires in the evil professor's face!

Basil turned on another of Ratigan's men and conked him over the head with his magnifying glass. Dawson tripped the third villain and sat on him.

Seeing that his men had been overcome, Ratigan ran for the door before anyone could stop him. "I'll be back!" promised Ratigan as he disappeared into the thick London fog. "You haven't seen the last of me!"

Quickly Basil contacted Scotland Yard to pick up Ratigan's men. As for Countess Zenobia, she was very happy to see her sapphires again.

"Thank you so much," she cried. "I promise never to leave my door open again, and I've decided what to do with the jewels. I'm going to have them set into a lovely collar for my dog!"

Basil nodded politely to the countess and said good-bye. He was eager to go home and think up a plan that would let him catch that rat of all rats, a professor named Ratigan!

THE GREAT SHAPE UP

Everywhere you go, you see people walking and running and jogging and biking. Why are they all exercising? The reason is simple. Exercise can help you feel better and live longer. Keeping fit has been an adult craze for twenty years. Now experts are saying that kids need to exercise, too.

Too many young people sit around watching television and

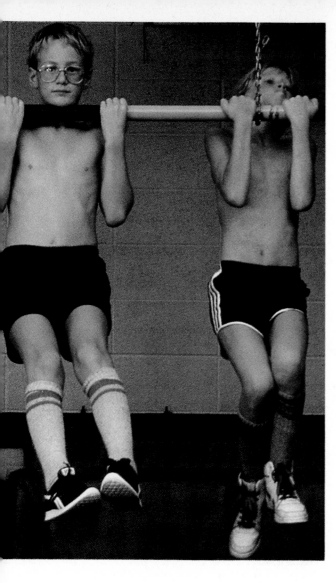

Kids who exercise do better at school. And they are often more confident, too. That's why many schools now have exercise programs that help kids improve their overall fitness. Chinning is only one of the exercises that can help you to stay healthy.

snacking. More children are overweight today than were overweight twenty years ago. So why haven't kids jumped on the fitness bandwagon? Well, most young people feel that they are pretty healthy. They don't think they have to exercise. "Don't we get enough of it in gym class?" they might ask. The fact is, the exercise you get in most gym classes isn't really enough to make you physically fit.

Many experts believe that if you begin to exercise when you are young, you'll be healthier throughout your life. Being fit can help you right away, too. Some California schoolchildren began to run for about a half hour every day. What do you think happened? They did better on school tests, and they were out sick for fewer days! Some experts even think that fitness makes children more confident. For these reasons, many schools are now adding activities that promote overall fitness as well as teaching sports.

You can improve your fitness on your own, too—or with friends. All you need is the right kind and the right amount of exercise. The right kind is one in which you keep up a steady movement over a period of time. This is known as aerobic exercise. "Aerobic" means "with oxygen." When you do aerobic exercises, oxygen is taken in by your lungs and carried by your blood to your muscles. Your heart works hard to keep the blood moving. Your heart is made of muscle. And like any other muscle it grows stronger with use. That's why aerobic exercises help

Aerobic dancing really gets your heart pumping—and it's fun, too.

Bicycling is another enjoyable activity that's also great exercise.

strengthen your heart. They also improve your general muscle tone and burn up calories, helping you to stay slim.

The really great thing about aerobic exercise is that there are so many ways to do it. You can run or jog. You can take a bike ride or go swimming. You can row a boat or go roller skating. Any one of these will give your heart and lungs a good workout.

How long should you exercise? That depends on how fit you are to begin with. It also depends on which exercise you choose. If you are badly out of shape, fifteen or twenty minutes of brisk walking may be enough. As your fitness improves, you can gradually make your workouts longer. Or you can start doing more strenuous exercising, such as running.

However fit you are, here are some tips that will help you avoid injuries when you exercise:

• First warm up. This will get the blood flowing to your muscles. Stretching exercises are good warm-up activities. Or if you are going to jog or run, start by walking briskly for a few minutes.

• Finish your workout with a few minutes of easy exercises, too. If you run, walk for a few minutes when you are done.

• Don't push yourself too hard. Do what's comfortable for you. Always increase your workload slowly. And anytime you feel pain, stop what you are doing.

As long as you are careful, exercise can only be good for you. So what are you waiting for? It's time to get off the couch, stop snacking, and shape up!

Running will give your heart and lungs a good workout. So unglue yourself from the TV and shape up!

MAGIC WITH MIRRORS

A kaleidoscope is magical. It turns simple objects into beautiful images. How does it work? Well, it's all done with mirrors!

The mirrors—there are two of them—are inside the tube of the kaleidoscope. The mirrors form a V. The light reflected from the objects at one end of the tube bounces back and forth between the mirrors. So when you look through the kaleidoscope's peephole, you see many images—the objects themselves, their reflections in the mirrors, and reflections of the reflections. But no matter how many images you see, the designs in a kaleidoscope are always perfectly balanced, or symmetrical.

The objects in most kaleidoscopes are bits of colored glass and beads. Some kaleidoscopes let you see other things as well. Just turn the page to see some of them.

A kaleidoscope has turned balloons, seashells, and flowers into fascinating patterns. Common pushpins explode in a colorful sunburst. Even a bunch of things that may be found in your desk drawer form a marvelous picture. Can you see the pencils, erasers, pennies, and stamps in the photograph at the top right?

THE PET PROJECT

"Come on, little buddies," Baloo called to Kit and Molly. "It's time to zoo-bee-doo to the zoo!" Kit and Molly came running. Molly wore her new jacket with the chrome buttons.

But before they could leave, Molly's mother, Rebecca, stopped Baloo. "A rush delivery just came in," she told him. "It has to go out today."

"Aw, Becky, can't it wait?" Baloo looked at Kit's and Molly's downcast faces.

"I'm sorry," Rebecca said, stroking Molly's head. "It's a load of ice blocks for Nostralia. They're having a heat wave, and they need the ice right away." But she did agree that Molly could go with Baloo and Kit.

Soon Baloo's plane, the *Sea Duck*, was landing at Nostralia's tropical airport. While Baloo and Kit helped unload the ice, Molly wandered to the edge of the jungle to sit in the shade. She took off her jacket and leaned against a tree.

Something tugged at her jacket. Molly sat up, her heart pounding. The something tugged again. Molly turned around carefully.

There was the strangest bird she had ever seen! It had a skinny neck, long legs, and knobby knees. Its wings were small and stubby, and its big, round body was covered with shiny feathers that looked like metal. And it was eating the buttons off her jacket!

"Stop that!" Molly grabbed her jacket, but the bird neatly nipped another button off! It looked so funny, Molly had to laugh. "You're cute," she said. "Want to be my pet?"

Molly led the bird to the *Sea Duck*. Baloo and Kit had finished unloading, and the hold was empty.

Quickly Molly led the bird inside. "You should hide until we're home," she said. Then she slipped into the cockpit with Baloo and Kit.

Soon the *Sea Duck* was rising skyward.

"Now, that's the kind of job I like," Baloo leaned back in his seat. "Easy and breezy!"

A loud clank from the cargo hold interrupted him. Kit jumped
up and opened the cargo door.

"There's a bird in here and it's eating the bolts on the door!"
Kit cried. "It's a nostrich. I've read about them. They can't fly,
and they'll eat anything. Especially anything metal," he added as
the nostrich happily gulped down another bolt.

"How did it get in there?" Baloo looked at Molly.

"It followed me, Baloo." Molly squirmed. "It ate the buttons on
my jacket. I thought it wanted to be my pet."

The nostrich waddled into the cockpit, smacking its beak as it swallowed two knobs and three dials from the control panel.

"Cut it out, you metal-muncher!" Baloo yelped. "No one eats my plane! I'm taking you back!"

"But, Baloo, it likes me!" Molly threw her arms around the nostrich's neck.

Baloo just shook his head and turned the *Sea Duck* around. Suddenly bullets rattled against the plane.

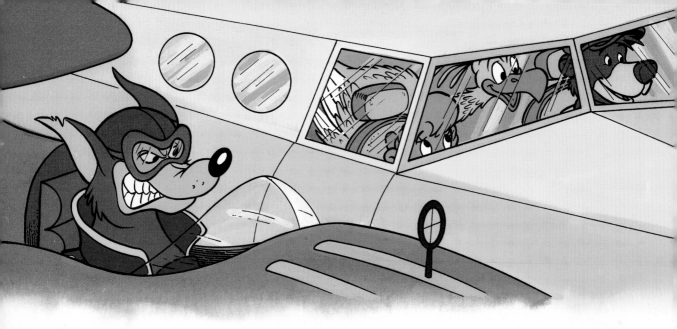

"It's Don Karnage!" Kit yelled.

"Hang on tight!" Baloo pulled back on the wheel, and the *Sea Duck* climbed, straight as an arrow.

But soon Don Karnage caught up with them. Looking into the *Sea Duck*, he saw the nostrich's shiny feathers. His eyes gleamed with greed.

"Hand over that valuable bird!" he cried.

"Come and get it," Baloo yelled back.

The pirate twirled a long rope with a pronged hook at one end. He flung it at the *Sea Duck* and the hook stuck in a wing. The plane tilted as the pirate climbed aboard.

"Give me that bird!" Don Karnage cried.

He was surprised when Baloo didn't argue. "Take it, Karny old pal," he said, hiding a smile.

With the nostrich under his arm, Don Karnage slid down the rope to his plane, unfastened the hook, and flew away.

"Baloo, how could you?" Molly began to cry. "Just think of that poor helpless little nostrich with that mean old Don Karnage!"

"Okay, okay," Baloo sighed. "But I wouldn't worry about that bolt-eating buzzard. It's not very helpless."

Baloo zoomed after Karnage's plane. "Just a few more minutes is all it should take," he said to himself.

Suddenly Don Karnage's plane began to swerve. It tilted, jolted, jerked, dipped, bumped, and spun.

"Is that crazy pirate trying to dodge us?" Kit asked.

"He's trying to dodge the nostrich," Baloo laughed.

They watched Don Karnage wave his arms and yell at the nostrich, which was climbing all over the plane, biting off large

chunks. As the *Sea Duck* crew
watched, Don Karnage's plane
began to fall apart.

"Hey, Karnage, need some
help?" Baloo called.

"Take back this preposterous
pigeon!" Don Karnage shook
his fist at Baloo and flung
the nostrich out.

"Baloo, it can't fly!" Molly
shrieked.

"Grab your airfoil," Baloo
commanded Kit. Kit opened his
airfoil and jumped from the *Sea
Duck*. He swooped down and caught

the nostrich. Holding it carefully under his arm, Kit trailed home behind the *Sea Duck* and floated to a gentle landing right behind it.

Baloo jumped from the plane. "I'm making one more delivery today," he declared, leading the bird away.

The next day, Baloo woke Molly and Kit early. "It's zoo-bee-doo-bee-doo day," he said, "and I've got a surprise for you!"

66

Baloo led Kit and Molly past the elephants and giraffes, past the alligators and flamingos, to a big wide field. There, behind an unchewable safety-glass fence, stood the nostrich.

"Now coming to the zoo will be like visiting a friend," Molly laughed.

Baloo grinned. "I just hope he never invites us to stay for dinner," he said, looking at the nostrich happily munching away at a big pile of shiny buttons and bolts.

THREADS OF SILK

In the story *Charlotte's Web,* by E. B. White, a beautiful spider named Charlotte A. Cavatica astounds everyone by spinning words. Real spiders can't do that. But they can spin an amazing material called spider silk—which is as strong as steel and as elastic as a rubber band.

Most spiders use their silk to build sticky webs that will

capture insects and other prey. But spiders are able to spin different kinds of silk, for many different purposes. They can spin a silk that is used as a kind of sandwich bag to keep the insect in until mealtime. To protect their eggs, female spiders wrap them in a soft cushion of still another kind of silk. And when the eggs hatch, each little spiderling spins a long streamer of silk. The wind catches the streamer and lifts the spiderling high into the air like a balloon on a string. Wherever the baby spider lands, it makes its home.

The Battle of Antietam was fought on September 17, 1862, in Maryland. It was the South's first attempt to invade the North. It failed.

THE CIVIL WAR
An Anniversary

The year 1990 marked the 125th anniversary of the end of the Civil War. This terrible war between the Northern states and the Southern states began in 1861. It ended four years later, in 1865.

Why did Americans fight Americans? Two issues tore the country apart in 1861: slavery and states' rights. There were many large plantations throughout the South. Black slaves did most of the work on them. In the North, farms were smaller.

There was little need for slave labor. Also, manufacturing developed earlier in the North than it did in the South. By the early 1800's, slavery had been outlawed in most of the North. By the mid-1800's, many people in the North wanted an end to slavery in the entire country. These people were called abolitionists because they wanted to abolish, or end, slavery. But Southerners felt that slavery was important to their way of life. And they believed that each state should have the right to decide for itself whether to have slavery.

In 1860, Abraham Lincoln ran for the presidency of the Union. He was the candidate of the Republican Party, which was against slavery. When Lincoln won the election, many Southerners were angered. Lincoln hadn't said that he would end slavery, but

In 1860, slaves made up almost a third of the South's population. They were often sold at slave auctions, such as the one shown here.

Abe Lincoln and the Great Debate

In 1858, Abraham Lincoln tried to win Stephen Douglas's U.S. Senate seat from Illinois. The two men debated seven times about slavery. Douglas said that each state should have the right to decide whether it wanted slavery. Lincoln said that slavery was evil. Lincoln lost the Senate race. But the debates made him well known. In 1860, the Republican Party chose him to run for the presidency. He won—and this set the stage for the Civil War.

Southerners believed he would do just that. As a result, in December, South Carolina seceded from, or left, the Union. Alabama, Mississippi, Florida, Georgia, and Louisiana followed soon after. These states formed a separate country—the Confederate States of America. Jefferson Davis was named president. Texas, Virginia, North Carolina, Tennessee, and Arkansas joined the Confederacy later.

Even though South Carolina had left the Union, the federal government still controlled Fort Sumter in Charleston Harbor, South Carolina. The Civil War began when Confederate forces fired on this fort, on April 12, 1861. The fort fell to the South

The Confederate flag flies over Fort Sumter, South Carolina. The war started when the Confederates fired on the fort, on April 12, 1861.

Nearly 200,000 blacks courageously fought in the Union Army. Many had been slaves. Black soldiers are shown here at a battle in 1864.

within two days. The South won several other victories, at first, too. One of the most important was the first Battle of Bull Run. Defeats such as this, just a few miles from Washington, D.C., made the North realize that this war would be long and hard.

In the fall of 1862, President Lincoln took an important step. He issued the Emancipation Proclamation. It freed the slaves in the Southern states. But the North didn't control the South, so not many slaves were freed immediately. (The Thirteenth Amendment to the U.S. Constitution outlawed slavery throughout the United States. It became law just after the war.)

The long, bitter war came to an end in 1865. Union armies had advanced deep into the South. In early April they captured Richmond, Virginia, the Confederate capital. On April 9, the Confederate forces surrendered. Just five days after the surrender, President Lincoln was shot and killed by John Wilkes Booth, a strong supporter of the South. The president's death was a tragedy. People had counted on him to help heal the wounds of war.

The cost of the Civil War was enormous. About 620,000 Americans died. And the economy of the South was shattered. But the Union was preserved. This enabled the United States to begin one of its greatest periods of growth and expansion. At the same time, blacks were freed from slavery. They were able to begin their long and difficult struggle for civil rights and equality.

Confederate General Robert E. Lee surrenders to Union General Ulysses S. Grant. The surrender, on April 9, 1865, took place at Appomattox Court House, Virginia. It ended the long and bitter American Civil War.

SCULPTURES IN THE SAND

Have you ever been to the beach and seen a sand sculpture contest? It wouldn't be surprising if you had. Sand sculpture has become "big"—in more ways than one. Imagine, for example, a sand castle nearly as tall as a four-story building and twice as long as a basketball court! Such a castle—called Bluebeard's Castle—was built at Treasure Island in Florida a few years ago. About 1,400 people worked for almost two weeks to build it. They used 20,000 tons of wet sand!

Castles are popular with sand sculptors. But they also make

ships, telephones, pigs, dogs, dragons, and sea serpents. At one contest, a team led by a dentist carved a set of giant teeth—along with a toothbrush and a tube of toothpaste.

Would you like to create a sand sculpture? Sand is easy to shape and carve, but start out with something simple. First, plan your design. Most sculptures are wider than they are tall. Then pile wet sand in the rough shape of the sculpture. Now you are ready to carve the final shape. You can use many kinds of tools for this—even a putty knife or a melon-ball scoop. While you are working, remember to spray water on the sculpture from time to time, so it doesn't dry out and crumble. Work as quickly as you can. All sand sculptures have short lives. Sooner or later the tide will come in and wash them away.

Sand sculpture contests are very popular. Thousands of people came to see this peaceful pig and chunky car—before the tides washed them away.

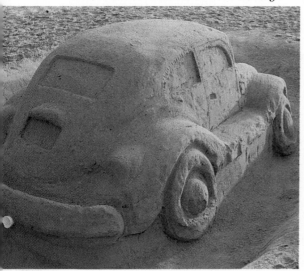

THE WATER WITCH

Once there was a place called Green Valley. It was blessed with fair weather, sunny skies, and gentle rain. The people who lived there were happy to live in such a wonderful place.

The children of Green Valley were happy, too, especially Calvin, Marvin, Melvin, and their little sister, Bitsy. They called themselves the Junior Knights, and they played all day at Great Adventures.

King Leo the Lazy lived in the big castle on the hill. Every day, people brought him baskets, barrels, boxes, and bushels of food. King Leo grew fat, happy, and even lazier.

Then, one year, the rain was late. The farmers waited for the rain to make their seeds grow. They waited, and waited, and waited some more. Still no rain came.

King Leo the Lazy waited, too, but the baskets and barrels and boxes and bushels of food didn't arrive. King Leo grew thin and mean—although he stayed very lazy.

The weeks without rain turned into months without rain, and then into an entire season without rain. The town well dried up,

and so did the lake. Things got so bad that King Leo the Lazy and his court packed up their belongings and moved away.

Calvin, Marvin, Melvin, and Bitsy, the Junior Knights, were sad to see King Leo and his knights leave. They feared there would be no more Great Adventures.

One day an old man came to Green Valley. "I can find water," he told the townspeople. He showed them a strange forked stick. He said the stick would point to water that was under the ground.

There was hope in Green Valley as the old man walked over town and farm, field and forest, waiting for his stick to twitch and tell him where there was water.

"It must be the Water Witch. She lives in that mountain," said the old man. "She stole the water of Green Valley. If you want it back, you must offer her a gift."

"What kind of gift?" asked Bitsy.

"No one knows," the old man answered sadly.

Day after day, nothing happened. The townspeople were about to give up hope, when suddenly the stick began to wiggle.

"Water!" shouted the old man.

The stick was pointing to a purple hill overlooking Green Valley. Then, all at once, the stick crumbled to pieces.

That afternoon the people of Green Valley held a meeting to
decide what to offer the Water Witch. The meeting went on far
into the night. The next
morning, the grown-ups
were still arguing.

"They'll be arguing
forever," said Calvin, "and
there's no time to waste."

So the Junior Knights
began hiking to the
Water Witch's mountain.
At the top of the
mountain they found the
entrance to what looked
like a small cave. "This
must be it," said Melvin.
"Are you scared?"

"Yes," said Calvin.

"Yes," said Marvin.

"Yes," said Bitsy. "But not too scared to try to save Green
Valley."

"Remember—this is a Great Adventure," Calvin said.

They walked into the cave and found themselves standing on a
narrow ledge. And they saw to their amazement that they were
in a huge cavern dripping with water.

"I've never seen so much water!" cried Calvin.

The floor of the cavern was a lake, and in the middle of the lake was an island.

In the middle of the island stood the Water Witch. She was all blue, an ugly, mean-looking blue. And the Water Witch was an ugly, mean-looking witch. She gazed up at the children.

"Visitors! How nice!" said the Water Witch. Then she waved her hand and the Junior Knights were whisked onto her island.

"Have a drink of water," offered the Water Witch. "It will probably be your last!"

The Junior Knights gulped hard. Calvin stepped forward. "Water Witch, we'd like our water back, please," he said, politely.

"I'll bet you would," answered the Water Witch. "What will you offer me?"

"My father's sword," said Calvin. He held out the shiny sword.

"What do I want with a sword?" asked the Water Witch. She pointed her finger and the sword crumbled in Calvin's hand.

The Water Witch turned to Marvin. "What will *you* offer me?" she asked.

Marvin rolled his eyes and swallowed hard. "I will offer you a kiss." He closed both eyes and puckered up. But instead of kissing him, the Water Witch threw a bucket of cold water in his face.

Then she turned to Melvin. "What will *you* offer me?"

Melvin reached in his backpack and pulled out a piggy bank. "All my money—every last cent," he said.

The Water Witch shook with laughter, splashing water on Melvin. "Money means nothing to me!" Then she turned to Bitsy.

"And what about *you* little girl?"

Slowly, Bitsy reached in her purse and pulled out a tattered old rag doll with one eye missing. "This is Esmerelda. She's my favorite friend," said Bitsy.

The Water Witch howled with laughter. "A doll! I won't give up my water for a doll! Now be off with you!" The Junior Knights turned to leave the cave.

Suddenly, Bitsy turned back to the Water Witch. "Here. You can keep Esmerelda, even if you didn't give us the water."

The Water Witch was shocked. "Why?" she asked.

A tear rolled down Bitsy's cheek. "Because I feel sorry for you, living all alone in this cave without any friends. Esmerelda can be your friend," she explained.

The Water Witch said nothing as she reached out to take the doll. The moment she touched Esmerelda, she turned into a beautiful blue princess.

"Oh, thank you!" the princess exclaimed. "Years ago, an evil wizard put the Curse of the Water Witch on me. The only thing that could break the curse was an act of true caring. How can I ever thank you?"

The Junior Knights looked at one another. Then all together they shouted, "You can give us the water!"

"Gladly," the princess laughed.

The people of Green Valley dug a hole through the mountain. And soon a waterfall streamed down the side of the mountain. The water quenched the people's thirst, watered their crops, and floated their boats.

The princess moved into the castle abandoned by Leo the Lazy and was loved by everyone in Green Valley.

The townspeople built a statue of Bitsy and her doll, to honor the little girl who had saved the town. It's all still there: Green Valley, the castle, the waterfall, the lake, and the statue. It's all still there—if you can find it!

LITTLE FLYING JEWELS

In a burst of brilliant color, a tiny bird appears. It seems to be standing still in the air. But its wings are beating. And they are beating so fast that they are nothing but a blur. Then it zips away, vanishing as quickly as it appeared. The bird could only be a hummingbird, one of nature's most fascinating creatures.

There are more than three hundred kinds of hummingbirds. Some live in North America. But most live in South America near the equator, where it's warm all year round. The bee humming-bird lives on the tropical island of Cuba. It's the smallest hummingbird—and the smallest bird—in the world. You really could mistake it for a bee. It weighs about as much as a penny and is just 2 inches long. And half that length is made up of its beak and tail! The largest hummingbird is the giant humming-bird. It lives in the Andes Mountains of South America. It weighs ten times as much as the bee hummingbird and is over 8 inches long.

In between the bee and the giant are hummingbirds of all sorts and sizes. But most of them are small. And many are beautifully and brightly colored. Hummingbirds can also be thought of as the acrobats of the bird world. A hummingbird will hover motionless in front of a flower to sip nectar. When it is done, it will actually

Hummingbirds build their nests out of bits of plants, moss, and spider silk. The tiniest hummingbirds can sit atop a pencil eraser.

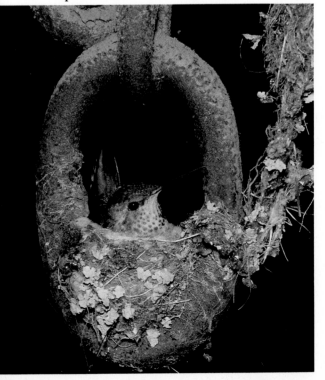

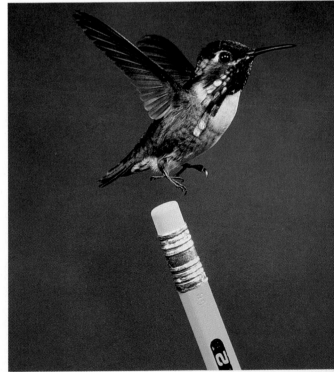

fly backward to withdraw its bill from the bloom. It will then dart a few inches to the side and hover again. Then it will suddenly dart away, reaching a speed of 30 miles an hour almost immediately. Hummingbirds can even fly *upside down* for short distances.

Most hummingbirds have long, thin bills. They use these to sip their favorite food—the nectar of flowers. Hummingbirds also eat tiny insects and spiders. And they like spiders for another reason. They steal bits of spider webs to use in building their tiny nests.

Female hummingbirds usually lay two tiny eggs. They raise their chicks on a diet of insects. Birds of prey would be wise to

Hummingbirds in Your Garden

To attract hummingbirds to your garden, just plant some of their favorite red flowers. Try trumpet honeysuckle and fuchsia. Or put out a nectar feeder. You can make one from a small bottle. Fill the feeder with a solution of one part sugar to four parts water.

A hummingbird seems to be motionless in front of a flower. Actually, its wings are beating so fast that they are just a blur to the eye. How fast? The wings of some hummingbirds beat 80 times a second. This rapid beating creates a humming sound—and that's why these wonderful creatures are called hummingbirds.

stay away from hummingbird nests because these tiny birds defend them with amazing courage.

Spanish explorers saw hummingbirds when they first arrived in the New World from Europe. One explorer wrote that "The colors shine like those of the little birds artists paint to illuminate the margins of holy books." They are, indeed, beautiful birds. In fact, hummingbirds are famous for their vivid tones—green, blue, ruby, violet, magenta. The brilliance of the birds' feathers has led people to call them "flying jewels." One day you might be lucky enough to see one of these tiny gems hovering over a flower right in your own backyard.

HERE COME THE ROLLER-BLADERS

Roller-blades are like ice skates with a single row of wheels. And a roller-blader can glide like an ice skater —but in summer.

It's summer. There's no ice, so you can't go ice skating. There's no snow, so you can't go skiing. But you can match the fun and thrill of these sports. Just grab your roller-blades and head for the park or some other place with a smooth pavement.

Roller-blades are like regular roller skates, but with one big difference. Roller skates have two sets of side-by-side wheels. Roller-blades have three, four, or five wheels one behind the other, in a line, similar to the blades on ice skates. This is why roller-blades are also called "in-line" skates.

Once you get the hang of it, roller-blading is easy. You can glide like an ice skater or skier. And you can turn as easily as you would on a bike—just by leaning to whichever side you want to turn to. The hardest part is learning to stop. There's a plastic stopper at the back of one of the blades. To stop, you just drag the stopper along the ground. Make sure you practice this a lot.

Roller-blades were first developed in the United States about ten years ago. They were used mostly by hockey players and skiers for summer training. Hockey players and skiers still go roller-blading to practice. And other people do it because it's a great way to exercise. But most people do it just for fun.

Whether you want to exercise or just have fun, here are some important safety tips:

• Always wear a helmet, knee and elbow pads, and wrist guards.

• Skate on smooth surfaces. Watch out for potholes, cracks, and other hazards.

• Stay away from slopes until you are really experienced.

• Skate slowly. You can increase your speed as you gain experience and confidence.

This boy is warming up for a game of roller-hockey. During roller-hockey games, players wear helmets and other safety equipment.